Dedication

Ronald Williams

This AASCU study is dedicated to, and inspired by, the memory of Dr. Ronald Williams, former president of Northeastern Illinois University.

President Williams was voted AASCU's Chairman-Elect in 1984 and was to have assumed the chairmanship in 1985. After his death in December 1985, he was named honorary AASCU Chairman for 1985-1986.

As president of Northeastern Illinois University from 1976-1985, Dr. Williams improved the general education and liberal arts base of all the university's undergraduate programs and oversaw development of new curricula in disciplines designed to meet society's most pressing contemporary needs. In particular, he recognized the important role of urban universities in reaching out to minority populations.

Born in Cleveland, Ohio, Dr. Williams received a Bachelor of Arts in speech and hearing and a Master of Arts in speech therapy at Case Western Reserve University. He earned a doctorate in phonetics and psycholinguistics at Ohio State University. He served on the faculties of Ohio University, Oberlin College, Western Washington University, the University of Pittsburgh, and the University of the District of Columbia, where he was provost.

This study, and all of AASCU's ongoing efforts for educational equity, are a continuation of Dr. William's lifelong commitment to minorities and public higher education.

i

Minorities in
Public Higher
Education

At a Turning Point

 Press
Washington, D.C.

Support for the publication of this book was provided by *The* College Board.

Distributed by arrangement with
University Publishing Associates, Inc.
4720 Boston Way, Lanham, MD 20706
3 Henrietta Street, London WC2E 8LU England

All AASCU Press books are produced on acid-free paper which exceeds the minimum standards set
by the National Historical Publications and Records Commission.

Library of Congress Cataloging-in-Publication Data

Minorities in public higher education.

Bibliography: p.
1. Minorities—Education (Higher)—United States.
I. American Association of State Colleges and Universities. II. Series.
LB2329.5.A43   378′.053   87-17554
|LC3731| 378′.1982
ISBN 0–88044–083–X (paperback)
ISBN 0–88044–093–7 (hardback)

Contents

Introduction

This study addresses the fundamental issues confronting public higher education in its efforts to reach America's minorities. It surveys higher education's historical progress in providing a path to equality and examines some disturbing recent trends that show a clear reversal of that progress. Each author offers strategies for stopping the trend and reawakening our national commitment to providing higher education as a path to equality for all.

In chapter 1, Clifton Wharton advocates a "second front" in the battle for educational equity. We as a society must augment past efforts such as affirmative action and judicial activism, because the statistics clearly show they are not enough. The key to the next wave of progress is to enhance the resources and values of the minority communities themselves. These communities must be the foundation for minority progress.

John Maguire expands on this theme in chapter 2. He argues that before any progress can be made, all of society must recognize its vital stake in minority progress. There can be no success if the problem is seen as a "we/they" problem. Moreover, this new perspective must be permanent. Previous gains were based on temporary attitudes, and those gains were then lost. Once society adopts a new, permanent point of view higher education institutions, state colleges and universities, in particular can be the path to "unity through multiplicity."

In chapter 3, Albert Whiting examines the historicial and contemporary vitality of traditionally black institutions. Through a series of interviews with college presidents, he explores the necessity and value of traditionally black institutions in a society committed to integration. He posits that the diversity of educational opportunity they offer will continue to be needed in our society's increasingly complex future.

1

Public Higher Education and Black Americans: Today's Crisis, Tomorrow's Disaster?

Clifton R. Wharton, Jr., Chairman of the Board and Chief Executive Officer, TIAA-CREF, and Former Chancellor, State University of New York

From a speech delivered in San Francisco at the National Urban League Conference on July 21, 1986. Used by permission.

Since our country's colonial days, education has been the keystone to progress. Yet growing numbers of American blacks appear indifferent, apathetic, or cynical about schooling and higher learning. Are they experiencing a crisis of faith in education as the privileged pathway to the future?

Minorities in particular have been ardent believers in education as central to the uniquely American belief in bettering one's lot in life. That it was once a criminal offense to teach a Mississippi slave to read and write was no accident. Nor was it a coincidence that so many black heroes during slavery were heroes of literacy, such as Frederick Douglass. They realized that freeing their minds was the first and most important step toward freeing their people.

Since then, the quest for educational opportunity has been largely indistinguishable from the quest for freedom and justice. Education and equality, knowledge and power: more often than not, these goals have been one and the same for America's disenfranchised. They were one at the ground breaking of Tuskegee Institute and Howard University. They were one and the same in Little Rock, and at Ole Miss, and at the University of Alabama. They have been one in Detroit, in South Boston, and even in the lecture halls and anatomy labs of the School of Medicine of the University of California, Davis.

All this has been true to a greater or lesser degree for a vast cross section of Americans: working-class whites ... women ... the first waves of European immigrants, and later Asian, Middle Eastern, and Latin American ... and surely for almost every ethnic group that has sought to carve out a place for itself in our nation.

It has been especially true for we blacks—which may be another way of saying that if we have cherished education more, needed it more, it is because the blanket of bigotry upon us has been even coarser and more smothering than that cast over other groups. And the struggle has been longer because our first ancestors came to these shores before the Mayflower!

For blacks, increased access to education coincided with the advance of material progress and civil rights. Among the first triumphs

3

was the rise of independent black academies, technical training institutes, colleges, and professional schools. But in the South, "separate but equal" placed a major constraint on achieving true quality and equality in our public schools. Jobs and education for their children were the dominant drives for those early black migrants from the South to the North during the post-Reconstruction era and before World War I. Thus, until the end of World War II, blacks participated with only limited success in this century's accelerating trend toward universal schooling.

Then, with the coming of the GI Bill, black Americans' pent-up demand for knowledge began to escape its confines, before being explosively released in 1954 with Brown v. Topeka Board of Education. The fraction of blacks completing high school increased from 10 percent in 1940 to 70 percent in 1980.[1] As late as 1965, black enrollment had multiplied nearly four times, to 1,138,000.[2]

Until the 1960s, most of the growth in college enrollment took place on the campuses today called traditionally or historically black. After that, the momentum of black enrollment gains swung to the predominantly white—and especially the large public—institutions. In 1960, about 96 percent of all black college students were in 105 traditionally black institutions; by 1984, the figure had fallen to 19 percent.[3] Today, two-thirds of all black college graduates receive their degrees from predominantly white campuses.[4]

The Emerging Crisis

Why, then, are many educators convinced that something has gone very, very wrong in education for blacks, if not for other minorities? Why do I call it a crisis with disaster in the wings?

In recent years the pace of black gains in education has fallen sharply and in many areas has reversed itself. The percentage of blacks enrolling as full-time undergraduates peaked in 1978 at 10.6 percent. Thereafter there has been a gradual but steady drop each year. In 1984, the total enrollment of blacks at all levels was a mere 8.8 percent.[5]

What is going wrong? For blacks as well as others, the pool of college-age young people is shrinking—the "baby bust" is much less among blacks and Hispanics than among any other group of 18-to-24-year olds. Our percentage participation rates in college are declining.

4

Second, the percentage of black high school graduates who go on to college has remained high and roughly comparable to the figure for other segments of the population. For example, in 1980 the black high school completion rate nationwide was about 70 percent—much better than a generation before, but still substantially lower than the 83-percent rate for white youth.

But these figures are cruelly deceptive because they hide a profoundly negative factor: the obscenely high dropout rate in our schools. The overall 30-percent dropout rate for black students nationwide soars to 40 percent, 50 percent, and even higher in many central cities.[6] With these distressingly high rates, little wonder that so many of the few who are left go on to college.

Among black students, dropping out starts as early as the primary grades and extends right through high school. In some urban areas, it has reached and passed crisis proportions. As for those who do graduate, many are academically underprepared as a result of attending classes in which keeping order has displaced rigorous instruction. Some students will have been automatically "tracked" into vocational rather than college preparatory programs, regardless of their aptitudes and abilities. Others still will have been programmed to blame themselves for the failures of the educational system and will have come to hate the very idea of further study.

So much for our high schools. How do we fare in our colleges and universities?

At the postsecondary level, the pool of black youth eligible for college increased by nearly 20 percent during the last half of the 1970s—but the number who actually enrolled barely held steady.[7]

As mentioned, the percentage of black high school graduates who enroll in college is not much lower than for whites, but the dropout rate has so reduced the pool of high school graduates that black young people participate in higher education well below their race's representation in the citizenry at large.

Once enrolled in college, blacks are significantly less likely than whites to complete a baccalaureate program—the dropping-out trend does not end with the primary and secondary schools. Thus, the

5

educational pipeline that is squeezed at the primary and secondary level is squeezed even further in college.

At the graduate and professional level, things look even worse. As early as 1976, the proportion of blacks in graduate and first-professional programs had begun to fall from the already discouraging levels of the early 1970s.[8] Although blacks make up 12 percent of the U.S. population, they receive only about 5 percent of doctoral degrees annually.[9]

What makes the situation gloomier still is that far too few black graduate and professional students are entering fields that promise the greatest opportunities for the decade ahead. In 1984, 1,049 blacks in the U.S.A. received doctorates, but over two-thirds of them were in education and the social sciences.[10] What about the high-demand fields? National statistics indicate that blacks received fifteen Ph.D.'s in engineering, thirteen in business administration, eleven in physics, four in mathematics, and three in computer science. With these numbers, where will we get tomorrow's black teachers and professors for our colleges and universities?

When the black college enrollment is separated into male and female, a shocking picture emerges of even more massive enrollment declines for black males. Black women already outnumber black men on college campuses by a substantial margin—in New York, for example, black women outnumber men 5.3 percent to 2.7 percent.[11] Black male graduates are starting to become an endangered species.

Questions

Statistics such as these raise disquieting questions.

- Have we as a people lost our faith in education?

- Don't we *believe* any more that schooling is the key that opens the locked doors—or if need be, the battering ram that knocks them aside?

- Why, after having won at such terrible cost the right for our young people to attend school, has today's dropout rate reached the point of national educational emergency?

- After a sustained period of progress, why has black college enrollment stalled or even begun to decline at virtually every level?

- How will or can we correct for these massive losses in black human capital—all those who were squeezed out of the educational pipeline?
- Does society realize the enormous it will ultimately face by failing to avert the imminent disaster?

These are deeply troubling questions. And many of the answers are just as troubling.

First, there has been a major shift in public attitudes about equal opportunity, and especially about affirmative action. Not that long ago, there was a broad consensus about the nation's need for atonement to blacks and other minorities by taking positive steps to reverse the harm inflicted by past abuse and lingering discrimination. Today, the National Urban League is one of the few remaining strong, biracial organizations, and the U.S. Attorney General and even some members of our national Civil Rights Commission offer up statements that would reverse decades of progressive thought and action.

Many of our fellow citizens seem to believe that the need for affirmative action is past.

That affirmative action *has* made inroads is clear to most of us. But it is also clear that thirty years of affirmative action has been barely a first step toward eliminating our country's 300 years of racism and discrimination. We need steps two, three, and four down the road toward full equality. And until we get there, the old vicious cycles will remain pretty much intact. Disenfranchisement breeds poverty, which breeds bad neighborhoods, which in turn breeds bad schools and dropouts who can't get jobs. Unemployment breeds crime and welfare dependency and homelessness. Before long we're right back where we began. Only now we have a new generation seared with the permanent brand of oppression, locked permanently into what the sociologists have begun to call the "hard-core underclass."

None of this is really news. And yet I must say that there is a sense in which this analysis, so familiar and so intellectually comfortable, is nonetheless unsatisfactory.

It is only partially adequate to explain skyrocketing dropout rates and the erosion of black gains in higher education. And it is unsatisfying because it raises the further question of why, two or three generations ago, blacks somehow managed to advance educational goals even

though the decks were stacked even more formidably against them. The history of the National Urban League documents this. Many black adults today know that the barriers were much higher, the falls much harder—because they climbed the walls, they slipped and fell—and they rose to climb again. Whatever the remaining external, institutional barriers to education for blacks today, they are on the whole fewer, and lower, than ever before. School integration is the law of the land. Overt discrimination in college admissions is practically unheard of. Even in its subtler forms bigotry plays much less a part in the life of the typical campus than it did a short generation ago.

For the capable but underprepared, there are high school equivalency programs and developmental programs. For those economically in need, there are programs of financial assistance. Despite the hostile rhetoric of the current Administration in Washington, the actual availability of federal financial aid has so far been only slightly curtailed. And while there is a growing barrier resulting from higher debt levels caused by more aid in the form of loans, the fact is that finances are not a major obstacle.

Are persistent poverty and persistent discrimination obstacles to learning? Of course. Do delinquency, broken homes, alcohol and drugs, street culture, shoddy career counseling, youth unemployment, teen-age pregnancy, and all the other enduring pathologies of disenfranchisement contribute to today's dropout crisis and eroding college participation rates? No doubt.

But are they the root of the entire problem? That's another question. A harder, more complex, more intimidating one. And—let's face it—a much touchier one. Touchier, because it may bring us face to face with other challenges, arising not altogether from discrimination, but at least in part from changes in the psychology and value system of the black community itself.

I have no use whatsoever for the current ideological fad that goes by the tag of "blaming the victim." I do not intend to claim that we as blacks have become the source of our own problems. I do want to suggest that in education as in other important areas, black problems have evolved into issues that cannot be resolved *solely* by traditional, institutional, "civil rights" approaches. If that is indeed the case, we have an increasingly urgent obligation to explore additional, currently neglected avenues for change.

Self-Image, Aspiration, and Achievement

If you took a sample of black college graduates from the 1920s, '30s, '40s, and '50s, you might be able to put together a kind of composite personality profile. I haven't done anything so systematic. But I have talked with and known more than a few of them. I've met them in business and industry, in politics and public service, in science and the arts. As a group, they form the backbone of faculty on today's traditionally black campuses, and serve on faculties and administrations of our public schools and predominantly white colleges and universities.

Diverse as they are in so many ways, I've observed that black college graduates from the '20s through the '50s tend to share several key psychological features. They have a strong sense of self and heritage. They are family oriented and often community minded. They have tremendous drive and ambition. They know what they want to do. All they want to know is what it will take for them to do it. In a word, the blacks who attended college in the '30s, '40s, and '50s were and are people who *aspire*. And if their aspirations sometimes seem unrealistic to outside observers, well, just stand aside and watch.

They knew they had to be twice as good as their white peers to compete successfully, but they had the self-confidence to respond to that challenge.

How does this compare with the situation facing today's black college student?

Most college campuses use a set of euphemisms. One is "educationally disadvantaged." Another is "academically underprepared." Yet another is "full-opportunity admit." By and large, these clumsy, unlovely phrases are almost universally interpreted to mean one thing: "black."

The reverse is also true. Ask any faculty senate or administrative committee about black students, and they will immediately begin to tell you more than you could possibly wish to know about special admissions tracks, free tutoring, developmental counseling, remedial

reading labs, and all the other pedagogic paraphernalia associated with—not to put too fine a point on things—academic deficiency.

These views ignore the fact that many black students meet the same standards as other students, without the slightest need for outside help or special dispensations. They ignore the fact that on most predominantly white campuses, nonminority students far outnumber the minority in remedial classes.

They ignore, in other words, the facts. No, the link between blacks and deficiency is as unthinking, as reflective as the link between deficiency and blacks. It is a stereotype, but it is a stereotype that has taken on a life of its own. It lives in the press. It lives in Hollywood and on TV, where—"The Cosby Show" to the contrary—the story of blacks is too often the story of an unwed, illiterate mother, a violent coke dealer, an abusive wife beater, or a slightly buffoonish sidekick for a white superhero.

The stereotype also lives in the speeches of too many of our black officials and political figures, for whom antidiscrimination and antipoverty programs are perennial issues, while industrial development and national trade competitiveness are somebody else's problem.

And most to the point for this discussion, the stereotype is alive and growing stronger every day in the minds of our black young people.

Through images, representations, the very structure of language, our society sends an overwhelming signal to today's black youth. And the signal is: "Excellence is for other folks. Not you." In one breath we decry Jensen's idiotic theories of black intellectual inferiority; in the next breath we act as though he might be right.

I would like to be able to say that education is an exception to this corrosive assault, but it is not. From the first day of the first grade, to the moment when the last strains of "Pomp and Circumstance" fade into silence, many and perhaps most of our schools, colleges, and graduate institutions beat the same dreary drum.

Start in kindergarten. Set up "slow" classes to homogenize the classrooms. Pass the "slow" kids anyway, whether they've learned the material or not. Just make sure they know they're getting by "because they're black."

Design "aptitude tests" and academic tracking for the "culturally impoverished."

Hire guidance counselors who automatically, even benignly, steer black youngsters away from college, toward jobs immediately after high school, or at best toward technical curricula leading to jobs with low ceilings of advancement.

Demand dual college admissions standards—better yet, lobby for a tacit but real lowering of academic standards for graduation, graduate school admission, and professional certification.

And so on.

It is all reverse discrimination, in the only sense of that foolish phrase with any real meaning: discrimination by default, discrimination as the abdication of responsibility.

Do we think that by these shabby devices we're doing black youngsters a service? A *favor*? No. What we are doing is telling them, in a hundred whispered or unspoken ways each day, that we do not really believe in them. Is it any wonder so many of them are unable to believe in themselves?

It is hard to determine, and even harder to prove, just how thoroughly the individual's abilities to compete, to excel, and to achieve are shaped by self-image—which is, of course, closely tied to the perceptions and expectations of the individual exhibited by others. But there is a large and growing body of empirical research data supporting the common-sense view that self-respect is critical to self-realization.

In a recent issue of *New Republic*, two black writers summed it up as follows:

> Negative expectancy |among black youth| first tends to generate failure through its impact on behavior, and then induces the individual to blame the failure on lack of ability. . . . The misattribution in turn becomes the basis for a new negative expectancy. By this process the individual, in effect, internalizes the low estimation originally held·by others. . . . |This internal low expectation| powerfully affects future competitive behavior and future results.[12]

Over the last several years, I have nursed a growing conviction that one of the most urgent needs for black youngsters is a broad-based effort to foster stronger, more competitive, achievement-oriented self-images.

The need is by no means universal. Studies undertaken by Professor Walter Allen at the University of Michigan show the other side of the coin. His 1982 survey of 902 black undergraduates at eight predominantly white institutions showed that the students did not fit the stereotypical profile. Indeed, they held high aspirations and strong self-esteem: "Sixty-three percent . . . expressed 'above average' or 'high' levels of self-confidence. Most students, 59 percent, thought they were above average or high in leadership abilities. And 76 percent said that overall they were high or above average people.[13]

It takes only a moment's reflection to realize that these findings do not refute, but rather confirm, my larger thesis. For the fact is that Professor Allen's respondents were *not* the high school dropouts, *not* the youngsters who never enrolled in college, but rather the self-selected successes—the survivors. Already admitted to institutions with formidable academic standards, they represented the survivors of a war of educational attrition. And not surprisingly, they succeeded because they had good high school records and came from stable, well-educated, middle-class families.

Such youngsters are thus the classic exceptions who prove the rule. But the majority of their peers—the majority of our young people from kindergarten on—cry out for a massive infusion of self-esteem from our society as a whole, but most directly from the black community itself.

There are a few areas where they already have it. Nobody needs to set up remedial programs to get black kids into sports. In athletics, they know they can compete and even dominate. They see it for themselves, on every TV network. I'm not indulging the stereotype here for my own purposes. I'm trying to illustrate the effects of expectation on self-image and standards of performance. For unless you hold the dubious belief that blacks as a group are innately and overwhelmingly superior to whites as athletes, you are forced to conclude that sports are a field we have excelled in because sports are a field in which we *believe* we can excel. And our youth are willing to work long and grueling hours of practice and study to measure up.

Where is our comparable "intellectual competitiveness"—our "intellectual work ethic"?

The Role of the Family

If you look carefully at the matter, you will find strong self-images and driving personal aspirations most deeply rooted in tight-knit, supportive, and—indeed, yes—demanding families. — Such families were a prominent part of black America during the first half of this century. Their presence probably goes a long way toward explaining how those black high school and college graduates of the '30s, '40s, and '50s could accomplish so much, even against such appalling odds. Recently many of us have begun to ask again about the role of the family and the critical importance of the values embodied in strong families—discipline, hard work, ambition, self-sacrifice, patience, and love.

It's easy enough to mock such values as bourgeois. But middle class or not, they increasingly appear to constitute the spiritual foundation for achievement—the psychological infrastructure, if you will, for both personal growth and full participation in the world.

If you don't think such values are vital for intellectual growth, let me refer you to a recent study comparing the reading and mathematics skills of first and fifth graders in the United States (Minneapolis), Taiwan (Taipei) and Japan (Sendai). The sample included 1,400 students in the three countries. Its central finding was that American students scored lower, did less homework, spent less time in school, and were more likely to engage in irrelevant, nonacademic activities while in class. But the study also noted the pivotal role of family values. American parents, it seems, now place less importance on homework and are less likely to push their children to achieve than are parents in Japan and Taiwan. The researchers speculated that the old American work ethic now appears to appeal more to Asians than to Americans themselves, at least insofar as it pertains to basic schooling.[14] No wonder the newest Asian immigrant children are winning all the prizes.

Black gains in education and elsewhere have stalled at a time when the black family as an institution has been under severe stress. That is no coincidence. And so I must urge the rehabilitation of the black family as an institution for the transmission of sound values.

It is difficult to know all that such a job entails, or how we might do it. But even given the reservoir of good faith and commitment that still exists among many whites, it is a job that the black community must

undertake largely for itself. It is a job that requires us to look mainly inward, to our own needs and potential, rather than exclusively outward for assistance or reparations. And it is a job that calls for resources of creativity and strength that our own history documents in inspiring abundance.

The Need for a "Second Front"

Again, let me emphasize: I am not among that small group of blacks who have gained recent attention for their indifference and even their disdain toward affirmative action and other forms of civil rights activism.

We have a full unfinished agenda covering the entire educational ladder. On one end, for example, we need to fight for per-capital pupil expenditures in our black inner cities that will at least equal those in our white suburbs. At the graduate level, we need many more programs like the recently announced $9-million program of the Ford Foundation to increase the pool of minority doctoral students.

The day for affirmative action is far from past. Realism compels us to recognize that it will be a long time before we have exhausted the need for legislative remedies to injustice and regulatory reform of institutions. Nor have we reached a point where we can, even if we wanted, move forward without our white compatriots' ongoing commitment. Yes, we need leaders and friends like David Kearns, Ralph Davidson, Coy Eklund, Bill LaMothe, John Akers, and Don Keough. The help of thousands like them are essential if we are to achieve our ultimate goal.

But realism also compels us to recognize that for a growing segment of the black population, despair has acquired a self-sustaining momentum. Welfare dependency, crime, unemployment, illegitimacy, and many other social pathologies arose initially from systematic disenfranchisement; today, they no longer require the negative energies of overt external discrimination to keep them running.

To confront and reverse these pathologies, we need something new. We need strategies not to replace affirmative action and judicial activism, but to augment them. While pressing the traditional lines of attack, we also need to open a second front.

14

We need to strengthen the black family, particularly in communities where its structure and roles have been progressively eroded over the last generation.

We need to reassert the relevance of self-respect and high aspiration, and we have to persuade black youth that they can compete on equal terms not only in athletics and a few other circumscibed fields, but in fact across the whole spectrum of human striving—including the intellectual.

Above all, we need to ask more of our own leadership. We have to call upon the growing cadre of black leaders in business, labor, science, the arts, and education, as well as the traditional black leaders in the churches and government. We must ask them to tell the country that the black agenda is more than guarding black "turf" or constantly repeating the litany of only black issues.

In addition to national black leaders, we need more national leaders who are black. We need to remind our country that the war on poverty and discrimination is not just a black issue, but one that directly affects the material and spiritual interest of every American. And we have to insist that the black stake in America is a stake in the whole society. It is a stake in the full range of challenges and opportunities our country faces at the brink of the twenty-first century.

We need to open a second front, with a different set of strategies and tactics. The National Education Initiative adopted last year by the National Urban League represents a major opening volley on such a second front. I proudly congratulate John Jacob and the League for their nationwide crusade of educational renewal. Their five-year effort through the 113 affiliates harnessing each community's energies will prove to be a critical venture. I would particularly single out the League's "Math Count" program in Chicago because it seems to me very much a prototype of the kind of innovative, creative, and positive efforts that offer a new kind of promise. It is a program that builds self-respect and nourishes high aspiration among our black youth. It aims at fostering skills and abilities that remove the ceiling to upward mobility in society. But this is not the only program we should examine. There are others. We have heard of the outstanding efforts of Dr. Comer in New Haven and the CED program in Rochester. Each relies upon the only kind of

resources and commitment that have never failed us—the resources and commitment of the black community and its historic biracial coalitions, such as the National Urban League.

Turning Corners

Today's appalling school dropout rate and stalling of progress in higher education are only two aspects of what I believe to be an impending educational crisis for black Americans. It is a crisis that may, as I have suggested in the title of this essay, be transformed all too soon into outright disaster.

And yet despite everything—despite the unexpected problems and reversals of progress, despite all the broken promises and heartbreaking setbacks—my counsel is not, finally, one of despair.

I recall Langston Hughes's famous oft-quoted poem, "Mother to Son":

Well, son, I"ll tell you:
Life for me ain't been no crystal stair
It's had tacks in it,
and splinters
and boards torn up,
and places with no carpets on the floor—
Bare.
But all the time
I'se been a-climbin' on,
And reachin' landin's,
And turnin' corners
And sometimes goin' in the dark,
Where there ain't been no light.
So boy, don't you turn back
Don't you set down on the steps.
'Cause you finds it's kinder hard.
Don't you fall now—
For I'se still goin', honey,
I'se still climbin'
And life for me ain't been no
crystal stair.[15]

It's been no crystal stair for any of us.

But for all the tacks and splinters and bare broken boards, we have reached one landing after another. We see the proof of our ascent embodied in laws and institutions. We see it in our increased numbers in positions of prominence and influence. And we see it in matters less tangible, such as the strong, continuing support of enlightened white citizens for the National Urban League and other organizations devoted to justice and opportunity.

We've turned some corners, too. And it may be that we are turning another one, in asking ourselves whether we have an obligation to place the same high value as our fellow citizens on the fundamental American values of self-reliance and aspiration.

I said it before: again and again, the resources and commitment that have never failed us have always been those of the black community itself. They are rooted in an enduring faith that we *can* overcome—we *can* achieve our goal of full equality.

In the final analysis, *we* are the ones who can and who must eradicate the insulting and infinitely destructive equation our society continues to make between blackness and inferiority.

We are the ones who can and who must reassert the black claim on excellence—for our young people, no less than for ourselves.

After all the years of climbing, we know the weariness all too well. But we also know the perils of sitting down to rest.

And in these darkening years of our century's close, there are times when the illumination of truth and compassion seems to have flickered or even failed.

Must it be that we will have to light our own way?

If so, let our lamp be the lamp of learning . . . and let it burn brighter today than yesterday, and brighter tomorrow than today.

Notes

[1] Timothy S. Healy, S.J., Untitled address to American Council on Education/National Association of State Universities and Land-Grant Colleges (Denver: November 12, 1984).

[2] U.S. Bureau of the Census, U.S. *Statistical Abstract* 1985 (Washington, DC: U.S. Department of Commerce).

[3] Thad Martin, "Why Blacks Do Better at Black Colleges," *Ebony*, November 1984.

[4] Michael Nettles and Joan C. Baratz, "Black Colleges: Do We Need Them?" *Change*, March/April 1985.

[5] National Center for Education Statistics, *The Condition of Education*, 1985 (Washington, DC: U.S. Department of Education, 1986).

[6] Jeff Howard and Ray Hammond, "Rumors of Inferiority," *New Republic*, 9 September 1985.

[7] Susan T. Hill, "Participation of Black Students in Higher Education: A Statistical Profile from 1970-71 to 1980-81," National Center for Education Statistics Special Report 83-327, November 1981.

[8] Hill.

[9] Clifton R. Wharton, Jr., "The Minority Student Challenge," *Science*, 224.

[10] National Research Council, *Summary Report 1984, Doctorate Recipients from United States Universities* (Washington, DC: National Academy Press, 1986).

[11] New York State Education Department, *College and University Racial/Ethnic Distribution of Degrees Conferred, New York State, 1982-83* (Albany: SED).

[12] Howard and Hammond.

[13] Walter R. Allen, et al., "Preliminary Report: 1982 Undergraduate Survey of Black Undergraduate Students Attending Predominantly White, State-Supported Universities," Center for Afro-American and African Studies, University of Michigan, October 1984.

[14] Edward B. Fiske, "U.S. Pupils Lag from Grade 1, Study Finds," *New York Times*, 17 June 1984.

[15] Copyright 1926 by Alfred A. Knopf, Inc. and renewed 1954 by Langston Hughes. Reprinted from *Selected Poems of Langston Hughes* by permission of the publisher.

2

Reversing the Recent Decline in Minority Participation in Higher Education

John Maguire, President
Claremont University Center and Graduate School

Education is perhaps the most important function of state and local governments. . . . In these days it is doubtful that any person may reasonably be expected to succeed in life if he is denied the opportunity of an education. Such an opportunity is a right which must be made available on equal terms.
—*Justice Earl Warren, 1954*

In life as well as literature, point of view can be determination.

It is more than a rhetorical or psychological gimmick to view the status of the nation's minorities—especially potential students within those ranks—as a golden opportunity for America rather than a worsening crisis. Not only does the perspective of the "deficit model" tend to identify "the minority problem" as "their" not measuring up to "our" norms, but it distorts the reality of America. It suggests that "nonminorities" are and will continue to be in charge; that minorities will continue to constitute the minority when, in many regions of the country, they already constitute the majority in their age group; that unless minorities can meet today's often narrowly culture-bound standards—devised by others, too often administered without flexibility or sensitivity—they cannot proceed in the educational process; that "we" can have a sound academic process even when it is not "theirs" also; that the educational business of the nation can proceed as usual, with or without the successful involvement of minorities.

This perspective is wrong, and its consequences disastrous. When acted out, the participation in higher education of key minority groups—black and Hispanic, in particular—keeps declining, resulting in further underrepresentation of those minorities in our faculties and administrations. Increasing percentages of those groups become doomed to underemployment, dashed dreams, unrealized lives. Not only is society deprived of the contributions that, educationally empowered, they could make, but profoundly alienated, many of them stand in danger of becoming burdens to society—"tax eaters not tax payers," as Lyndon Johnson rather inelegantly used to warn. When the educational, social, and economic attainment of large segments of any nation's population is low, the cultural and economic life of that nation is adversely affected and, if the condition persists, placed in peril.

It is in the interest of all Americans—and, by extension, the world—that virtually all of America's citizens, irrespective of background, have

the opportunity to participate in higher education. That means, of course, being appropriately prepared for college, then sustained as needed—socially *and* economically—while students, and finally, assisted in securing respectable employment. If this is to occur, increasing minority presence and success in college must become a front-burner issue, and equity for all of our citizens must reemerge as an urgent, primary national goal.

Such facts and their causes urgently require a new perspective on and a quickened commitment to the higher education of minorities. Every dimension of our society must be involved: government at all levels, business (through alliances with educational institutions and corporate benefaction), private philanthropy (primarily foundations), and the educational system as a whole.

The Facts: Backsliding, Not Progress, on the Road Toward Equity

If the 1968 Kerner Commission were reporting today, its members would, given the prophetic tone of their study, no longer warn of the dangers of "*two* nations in America, one black, one white," but of those resulting from the many "nations" now constituting America. While for many years blacks, soon joined by Hispanics (Puerto Ricans and Cubans in the eastern United States, Chicanos in the West), dominated national thinking about minorities, the term *minority* has for several decades legally included American Indian/Alaskan Native, Asian or Pacific Islander, and nonresident aliens. These five rubrics merely hint at the richness and complexity of the groups composing America's minorities—each with its own history, language, customs, aspirations, and attitudes.

Rather than rejoice that national awareness is being expanded and refined to include the more than 125 ethnic, racial, and language groups now residing in substantial numbers in this country, many one-time professed proponents of affirmative action have thrown up their hands and declared that the situation is too complex to fashion and pursue policies that address the entire spectrum. They note accurately that, throughout most of the 1960s and into the 1970s, most national reports, studies, and strategies to assist minority-group students assumed that the majority of such students were black.

This focus, even preoccupation, disregarded the fact that Cubans and other Latin Americans were streaming into South Florida, Puerto Ricans into New York, Asian refugees from Vietnam, Cambodia, and Laos into the Pacific coast and Gulf states, not to mention large numbers of immigrants from other parts of Asia—Japan, Taiwan, Korea—into all parts of America. Indeed, the most striking demographic phenomenon of all was well underway—the Hispanification of the United States, resulting in five states being dubbed "Mexican-American" and the prospect that in one of them, California, attributable principally to this Hispanic growth, minorities will constitute a majority shortly after the year 2000.

It is crucial, if minority recruitment, retention, and advancement policies are to be successful, that education leaders be aware of the differences—sometimes subtle, other times enormous—between groups. Language is a bearer of culture. Religion does shape one's world view. Life in some climes is conducted differently from life in others. People aren't alike. But certain realities are true for all; e.g., mastery of English is a requisite for full success in America, and numeracy (competence in computation) is central to modern life. It is most difficult to exhibit one's facility with concepts, one's understanding of the world's complexity, one's sensitivity to subtle and sophisticated issues without literacy and numeracy. These are *sine qua non* skills on the road to educational empowerment and social equity.

Policies to encourage the mastery of these areas may have to be framed at a high level of generality to cover and extend to *all* of America's minority groups. The successful implementation of these policies will be carried out by those committed to them, and increasingly experienced with the individual characteristics and differences of those they are designed to aid. Policies need to be tailored, adapted, and addressed to particular people with particular histories.

The complexity of the situation, far from serving as a justification for retreat from addressing it, only underscores the urgency of responding to its challenge.

What are the facts about minorities and American higher education? What is happening with respect to students, faculty administrators, and governing bodies?

The picture is sobering. In the 1960s, after so many decades of neglect, minority participation in almost every facet of higher education began to expand, slowly but steadily, and by the mid-1970s had made impressive gains over figures of a mere decade before. Today, however, it is starkly clear that the forward momentum of the 1960s and 1970s has been arrested and—worse still—retrogression is evident in many areas. The hard, fundamental reality is that while minorities continue to grow both in numbers and as a proportion of the U.S. population (now constituting about 21.3 percent), they remain underrepresented in higher education (constituting only 17 percent of the student population).[1]

Enrollments

Access to college is, of course, closely linked to graduation rates from secondary schools. During the 1970s, the percentage of blacks of ages eighteen to twenty-four who had completed high school rose sharply, from 59.5 percent in 1970 to 69.7 percent in 1980. (For whites, the comparable figures are 81.4 percent in 1970, rising to 82.5 percent in 1980.) Over this period of time, the percentage of whites of ages eighteen to twenty-four who were enrolled in college held steady at 32 percent. For blacks, however, a different pattern emerged. Only 26 percent of that age cohort was enrolled in college in 1970, but by 1975, the proportion rose swiftly to 32 percent—the same rate as for whites. By 1980, however, that parity had been lost; the percentage for blacks had regressed to 27.8 percent, resulting in only a small increase over the 1970 baseline.

Similarly, 35.4 percent of Hispanic high school graduates of ages eighteen to twenty-four were enrolled in college in 1975—actually a higher rate that for whites at that time. By 1980, however, the proportion had dropped steeply to 29.9 percent.[2]

The most current data available, aggregated for minority groups, show modest enrollment increases from 1980 to 1984. These gains, slender though they may be, are found in two- and four-year institutions, both public and private. Minority students are enrolled in two-year institutions at approximately the same rate (21.2 percent) as their proportion in the population at large (21.3 percent). But they are seriously underrepresented at the four-year institutions, especially private ones.

The overall gains, however, mask substantial fluctuations for different groups in their college-going rates during the first half of this decade. Across institutions, enrollment of blacks slipped 3.3 percent, while Hispanics and especially Asians, at least in part because of an increase in the age cohort for both groups, showed significant enrollment increases—12 and 33 percent, respectively.[3] Indeed, college enrollments for blacks peaked fully a decade ago, in 1976, and have not rebounded.[4] More disheartening, the enrollment picture for blacks continues to show losses in numbers.

In level of enrollment, the overall number of minority undergraduates increased by 2 percent between 1980 and 1984, and modest increases were registered for graduate and first professional degree programs. Once again, there is a striking variation among minority groups. On the whole, Hispanics and, particularly, Asians have increased their proportion of enrollments at all levels, while blacks, except in first professional degree programs, have lost ground. American Indian enrollments at the graduate level have slipped, while progress at the undergraduate and, especially, in first professional programs is evident. In all, increased minority enrollments in first professional degree programs constitute the most encouraging development in recent years.

One crucial aspect of the college enrollment picture is the pattern of attendance by type of institution. For most minority groups, matriculation rates are far greater at the two-year community colleges and vocational-technical institutes than at four-year institutions. Among all Hispanics enrolled in higher education, 54 percent are found in two-year colleges. Meanwhile, at research-oriented universities such as Chicago, Harvard, and Michigan, to name but a few, minority enrollments, which have never been robust, continue their recent decline.

Perplexing enrollment patterns can be seen most vividly in the most recent graduate school figures. The combined number of Asian, black, and Hispanic graduate students has not changed much from 1976-77 to 1984-85—up 1.6 percent. That frail increase, however, embodies wide swings among the major minority groups: substantial increases for Asians and Hispanics that barely offset a sharp decline in the number of black graduate students.[5]

Doctoral, Medical, and Legal Education

The number of doctorates earned by minorities rose to 2,831 in 1985, up by 376 (or 15.3 percent) over 1975 and by 87 (or 3.1 percent) over 1984. The *proportion* of doctorates earned by minorities increased from 9 percent of the total in 1975 to 11.5 percent in 1985. Seventy-eight percent of the 376 increase in doctorates earned by minorities is attributable to Hispanics. The overall increase of 15.3 percent for doctorates earned by minorities is attributable mainly to the sizable 10.4-percent *decrease* in the total number of U.S. doctoral degree recipients (defined as U.S. citizens and permanent visa holders).[6]

There have been both gains and losses in minority enrollments in medical schools over the past decade. The most encouraging development during this period has been an increase in the proportional representation of Hispanics and, most dramatically, Asians; Asian medical school enrollment jumped from 1.8 percent of all medical school students in 1974 to 6.4 percent in 1985. However, the proportion of blacks enrolled in medical schools declined somewhat over the decade.

Meanwhile, minority enrollments in law schools continued to rise sharply from 1980 to 1985: American Indians up 11.6 percent, Asians up 31.2 percent, blacks up 9.9 percent, Hispanics up 22.1 percent. Law degrees earned showed similar increases. For the four groups combined, the number of degrees rose by 318 (or 11.2 percent) in 1980-81 and 1984-85.

A further matter of serious concern in minority enrollment trends is the skewed distribution of earned degrees among the various academic disciplines. Although this phenomenon has numerous variations among minority groups, one feature in particular shall be noted here: among black doctorate recipients in 1985, almost half (48.5 percent) were earned in a single field—education. For American Indians, the proportion of doctorates in education was almost as great—42 percent. Tremendous contrasts among minority groups are evident in the proportions of doctorates earned in the physical and life sciences, and in engineering. For example, 66.6 percent of Asian doctorates are earned in those three areas, while for blacks the proportion is 16.6 percent and for Hispanics 27.0 percent. Conversely, only 6.3 percent of doctorates earned by Asians in 1985 were in the humanities, while 17.9 percent of doctorates earned by Hispanics were in the humanities. These patterns have many implications; in particular, they directly affect the pool of potential faculty members, especially at four-year institutions.

The loss of momentum in minority college enrollments and in degrees earned is particularly unsettling when viewed in the light of urban demographics. Consider that twenty-three of the twenty-five largest public school systems in the United States have at least 50 percent minority enrollment; in fact, the *average* minority enrollment in those big-city school districts is about 75 percent. When viewed this way, the disparity in college attendance by rates between urban youth and more affluent suburbanites is all the more apparent and distressing.

Faculty and Administrative Staff

Trends in the employment of minorities in higher education, both as faculty members and as administrators, reveal some progress. Minorities, except for blacks, were somewhat better represented in the ranks of full-time faculty members in 1983 than in 1977.

Upon closer inspection, however, the figures for blacks reflect divergent trends: increases in the number of black full-time faculty members at the two-year institutions, but significant decreases in their representation at both the public and private four-year institutions (-6.2 percent and -11.3 percent, respectively). Even the sharp overall decrease at two- and four-year institutions combined (-4.3 percent) does not adequately reveal the extent of the problem at predominantly white institutions. Of approximately 18,800 black full-time faculty members, about 8,200 teach at traditionally black colleges and universities, where they constitute about 68 percent of the full-time faculty. Accordingly, the 10,600 blacks among faculty members at predominantly white institutions constitute a scant 2.3 percent of the full-time faculty members at those institutions.

In the administrative ranks, slight increases in minority administrators were apparent by 1983 (blacks had increased to 7.2 percent of all administrative positions and Hispanics to 1.6 percent). Asian representation among all administrators grew more rapidly, though Asians occupied only 1.1 percent of all administrative posts and the proportion of American Indians remained essentially unchanged.

The Big Picture

All of the figures just cited reflect more complex developments and, by their very nature, ignore important differences when, for example, they lump together Cubans, Mexican-Americans, and Puerto Ricans under the "Hispanic" rubric, and Americans of Japanese, Chinese, Korean, or Vietnamese origin under the "Asian" heading.

Each distinction aside, however, an overall picture emerges with powerful clarity. The academic pipeline for minorities in America, from secondary schooling through doctoral study, is filling with obstacles that impede the once rapid progress toward a more just system of postsecondary education. While the numbers bespeak continuing progress along several fronts, progress on the whole has slowed and even turned into losses, particularly with respect to black participation in higher education.

Most American colleges and universities today, including the relatively lower-tuition public colleges and universities, are not increasing the participation of minority groups in higher education or facilitating the transfer of students from one level to another. The commitment of substantial resources to reverse downward trends is, at best, uneven and, on the whole, woefully inadequate.

Some Underlying Causes

After all of the proximate causes for the recession in educational involvement with the nation's minorities are surveyed—shifts in the mood of the national electorate, fluctuations in the economy, reactions to earlier efforts deemed excessive, the failures of the schools to prepare students for college, high dropout rates, early child-bearing by substantial segments of certain groups—the ultimate fact remains: white America has always had problems acknowledging people with marked differences—particularly skin color, language, and culture—as equals. We were a nation built upon oppression of the true native Americans, upon slavery of blacks, and upon segregation of most of the "different" others. As Clifton Wharton puts it, "America's historic legacy of discrimination is troubling in its obstinacy and its ability to regenerate itself in ever-new forms and structures."

Point of view ultimately accounts for practice. The 1960s and early 1970s proved that practice can change attitudes (at least for a while, and to a certain, albeit limited, depth), but if practice that promotes change is to persist, the changed perspectives and altered attitudes that inform it must become permanent. Only then will equity in access for America's minorities become genuinely institutionalized. Otherwise, alas, the retreats that have characterized the most recent years will continue. This is why, throughout this essay, I call for a permanently changed point of view.

What are some of the elements impeding the full involvement of minorities in American higher education?

By no means are all minority students poor, but an unacceptably large percentage of them are—and that poverty plagues their lives from infancy onward. If their empowerment, if equity, were primary national goals, their school classes would be smaller, not larger, than the norm, their school environments would be more, not less, inviting and hospitable, their extracurricular activities would be enriched, not impoverished, and they would be assigned the best-prepared, not the worst-equipped, teachers. The school would become an institution that would help offset, rather than reflect, the ravages of privation.

By no means are all minority students underachievers, but too many become so because of the absence of adequate support, outside as well as inside the classroom. While those closest to them, their families, may aspire for their achievement, too many others—their teachers, school officials, "majority" peers—too often harbor low expectations for their academic, economic, and social success, and too many minorities, in turn, respond by fulfilling those minimal, even negative, expectations.

It is hard to overestimate the role that language plays in the education of minority students and how quickly those showing difficulty with English get shunted into the lower tracks and remain there, reinforcing their problems with language and saddling them over time with the label "educationally disadvantaged." Labeling and placement condition society's subsequent attitudes toward and exchanges with them. The educational tracking that begins with skin color, accent, or

idiom enlarges into social tracking and hounds these minority students for too much of the rest of their lives.

By no means are all minority students culturally deprived, but the fact that they represent different cultures—about which most white Americans know precious little—prompts that assumption about most of them. Economic disadvantage keeps individuals of *all* backgrounds from enjoying many of life's "finer things." But lack of familiarity with "high culture" hardly means the absence of any culture. Minority students reflect and are the bearers of the often rich, complex cultures in which they are reared.

Hence it is the *circumstances* of many minority youth—particularly their economic deprivation and poor language skills—and the *attitudes* of what has been the dominant society toward those circumstances that shape the destiny of young minority-group individuals and make their getting into and through college so difficult.

On our campuses, minority students must survive a bewildering registration process. Although most campuses once had tutorial clinics, many have been disbanded under budget cuts. Some give freshmen credit for skills so long as they were integrated with the substance of disciplines, but no more. Except at the open-access institutions, freshmen gain admission only on the evidence that they are prepared to do "beginning college work." Forget that the indices and tests that determine that readiness may be culturally biased or questionable: the current system has seemed to work. Yet fewer minorities are here now than a few years ago. The stated reasons? Fewer are adequately prepared these days, and scholarship aid for them has decreased; in a time of relentlessly rising educational costs, the primary form of aid has shifted from grant to loan. "The Ivy-types get the best," an admissions officer recently asserted, "the historically black colleges get the black bourgeoisie, and the great mainstream just seem, under the circumstances, less interested in college."

Once on campus, a disproportionately large number of minority students are counseled into vocational and occupational areas—in contrast to general liberal arts fields—or into ethnic studies. Even in the liberal arts, however, they encounter the freshly reasserted hegemony of Western studies and are offered few courses that seek creative ways to weave into the curriculum diverse strands of tradition reflecting their heritages—few courses that seek to provide a historical understanding of the cultural origins of all. These students are quickly made to feel that the curriculum (however race-, tradition-, or class-bound) is sound and that *they* don't measure up. They too often sense that adaption and assimilation are the only routes to success.

When one adds to this scene what for many is an alien food service, a hastily organized set of student activities, social hang-outs that are *de facto* off limits to them, an inadequate supply of sensitive counselors, and supplementary academic assistance that is hard to come by, if available at all, is it any wonder that the attrition rate of some minorities at the college level is considerably higher than that of their classmates as a whole?

Consider this situation in the wider context of a society that only two decades ago outlawed some of the most pernicious discriminatory practices in relation to its minorities, and has only since then begun to bring home forcefully the practical, social, and legal repercussions of bigotry. In this academic year individual bias and overt institutional racism may have diminished, but forgetfulness, short-sightedness, and insensitivity on the part of faculty and administrators—more so than malevolence or conscious discrimination—remain the principal on-campus impediments to the enrollment and success of minority students and the appointment and promotion of minority faculty and administrators.

The national political mood, fueled by the current Administration, suggests that these disheartening developments are tolerable, indeed acceptable—hardly a matter of grave national concern or great social urgency. During the past few years there have been no new federal programs for minority-group students. Yet at the same time there have been explicit attacks on "bilingualism" and a reduction of scholarship aid programs for all students—a wide-ranging assault on affirmative action. A terrible extension of the terms "forgetfulness, shortsightedness, and insensitivity" at the national level is readily apparent. Is it any wonder that so many minority young people feel alienated, that "The System" doesn't want to include them, that "The Dream" is for somebody else?

What Can Be Done?

Setting history aside for the moment, America cannot be morally true to its defining ideals if it turns away from these growing groups of its citizens. "The Dream" dissolves if it cannot be realized by substantial numbers of America's peoples.

Pragmatically, America cannot afford to disregard its minorities, soon destined collectively to become the majority in several of its states. If we are to continue to be resourceful, competitive, and strong—state by state, and in the nation as a whole—we must have an educated populace. To be sure, successful education begins in the schools (an area where universities are—and must become more—centrally involved). But the role of higher education is fundamental in the educational empowerment of the nation's people.

Some key actions must be taken by various institutions in our society, including state colleges and universities.

The Federal Government

Too often the pace- or mood-setting role of the federal government is underestimated. When national governmental leaders criticize programs aimed at the achievement of equity, ignore the enforcement of laws designed to promote it, and reduce the funds necessary to realize it, leaders at other levels of our body politic—including those on campuses—read that as a signal that the brief interlude of America's concern for affirmative action has ended, that action-stopping indifference to "the minority issue" is acceptable. Even if the primary centers for effective action must distance themselves from Washington and move nearer the local campuses, the work of state and regional leaders is amplified and assisted immeasurably when signals at the national level support their efforts.

An enduring role of the federal government is to set a national agenda—to declare that the educational empowerment of the country's minorities is a national priority, and to sustain a tone of urgency and support for all efforts at every level. The federal government must convincingly declare that equity for all Americans is a primary national goal.

Because actions speak louder than words, an indispensable role of the federal government is to maintain substantial financial aid programs so that minority students can afford to attend college. This means grants, by and large, rather than loans. It means providing colleges with the funds for transitional programs to strengthen student language, mathematical, and scientific skills.

One of the more promising proposals raised during the recent round of efforts aimed at federal tax reform is that educational savings by low-income families be exempted from tax liability, providing a modest tax credit when such savings are utilized for payment of bona fide educational costs.

An up-to-date, comprehensive data base is indispensable. The federal government must continue to demand accountability from institutions on the ethnic composition of students, faculty, and administrators. Today, less reporting is required and less is being done. But without reliable statistics, we cannot know how we are doing as a nation, and we cannot as effectively insist on action.

Foundations

A reaffirmation is required by the nation's philanthropic foundations of the primacy and urgency of educating America's minorities. While a few foundations—among them, Ford, ARCO, Hewlett—have continued major grants in this area, the majority of foundations have turned their funding elsewhere.

Several kinds of grants are needed. Those that support efforts linking higher with primary and secondary education—the colleges and universities with the schools—need to become widespread. More fellowship programs for minority students, especially to underwrite their postbaccalaureate education, are sorely needed. A number of pilot programs have been conducted in the past, and new ones could be better tailored to meet the needs of the current situation, gathering up the strengths of previous programs and avoiding demonstrated weaknesses. Those that have been most successful could be used as models for a number of new ventures. Ample funds, well administered, are urgently needed.

States and Their Higher Education Systems

"Scale, the appropriate scale, is everything." E. F. Schumacher's comment surely describes higher education today. Although every segment of society can and must play a contributing role, there is mounting evidence that the most effective agent for ensuring that minority students enroll in college—and, adequately sustained, eventually graduate—is the individual state. Indeed, the challenge of engaging minority students cannot be met if left up to the federal government, foundations, or individual campuses. States can establish a more pointed and tailored agenda for their jurisdictions. They can provide appropriate incentives. They are better able to evaluate colleges' compliance with civil rights statutes and are best suited to push colleges to do more than national laws require them to do.

Because both the public schools and public colleges and universities are the creatures of their states, it should be possible for the entire educational system of a state to be viewed as a complex whole. The relations and the responsibilities of the schools to higher education and vice versa could be considered, and policies that reflect and address those relations could be fashioned, from preschool and junior high, to high school and community college through university. How each level affects the others could be assayed, and concerted approaches to education at all levels simultaneously advanced. For example, a major public-service program utilizing all the media could be initiated by the state to inform minority young people about the importance of college and how to get there. It could be segmented by language to get to young people "where they are." It could reflect a comprehensive, consistent, interrelated approach to education that begins "while they are young."

Although many institutions share in the responsibility of enhancing the position of minorities in society, the nation's state colleges and universities inescapably will play a pivotal role in that process. Historically, these campuses have been instruments of democracy, serving to promote social mobility by providing quality education at reasonable cost to countless young and older Americans. Few, if any, social organizations are better positioned to help shape a truly equitable society in which minorities can more readily penetrate middle-class America.

34

Because of this, several constructive possibilities become plausible. The first group of activities might be called "reaching out" or "linking"—a complex linking on a number of fronts between four-year and the junior and senior high schools and community colleges with high minority enrollments. Some examples:

- of prospective college students at the junior-high level onward and multiyear encouragement of those students (reinstituting abandoned tutorial programs in which college students work with lower-level students);

- a much tighter connection between "master teachers" in the schools and college-level prospective teachers, mutually focusing on the special educational needs of students in minority schools;

- college faculty working with school faculty on curriculum development and leading-edge subject matter issues with special reference to the real-life situations of the state's minority students;

- initiating "into-college" programs that begin at the high school level and that, successfully completed, guarantee college admission coupled with additional leadership training.

Such linking between colleges and schools would go a long way toward ensuring that those minority students in the schools who do need enriched curricular opportunities and instruction provided by teachers with superior abilities will get them.

The links between two-year and four-year colleges are especially crucial because over half of the nation's Hispanic and Native American students enrolled in college, and over 40 percent of the nation's college-enrolled black and Asian students, are enrolled in two-year colleges. If these students are not to be dead-ended, four-year colleges must cooperate with two-year colleges, particularly those with heavy minority enrollments, to:

- develop early identification and tracking programs designed to encourage two-year college students to persist and transfer into the four-year college;

- conclude field-by-field, discipline-by-discipline articulation agreements so that students enrolled in two-year colleges have the

certainty of immediate transfer upon completion into a four-year institution with "full standing," i.e., without loss of time or credit;

- develop "field groups" of faculty in both kinds of institutions, e.g., in biology, history, economics—any and all of the disciplines—to discuss issues and topics in the field and to make the transfer of students as smooth and efficacious as possible.

Another group of positive possibilities for state colleges and universities would begin during the final stages of the student admission process. They could be called "on-campus, student-oriented actions" and would include:

- seeking to increase the amount of aid available to minority students from low-income backgrounds by pressing legislation at all levels and by initiating college financial planning programs in cooperation with the financial community;

- ensuring flexibility in the otherwise rigid application of only quantified criteria for admission, relying additionally on interviews and earlier personal association with minority students and their teachers to provide important elements in the admission decision;

- operating summer "bridge programs" to provide beginning minority students with an orientation to college life, academic skills development, and opportunities to strengthen motivation. A counterpart program for transfer minority students might run simultaneously;

- recognizing that many minority students, once on campus, may need continued supplementary skills development. The establishment of ethnically heterogeneous "learning communities," where the most sophisticated diagnostic materials quickly disclose which areas in a student's "skills equipment" need most work, leads to subsequent strengthening or reinforcement through group activities and projects. These small, well-run communities begin with each student's array of skills, celebrating each student's strengths and progressing from there. (By paying special attention to those students who may arrive most alienated—most in need of signposts and links to their own importance, that is, their own humanity—the college may reeducate itself to the meaning of the humanities for everybody, and students will have a better prospect of emerging with demonstrable and marketable competencies;

■ promoting genuine, coherent pluralism throughout the campus, particularly in all phases of the curriculum. This includes maintaining ethnic studies, not as academic ghettos for certain minority groups, but as needed, inviting intellectual opportunities for all;

■ inventing subtle but real ways to support minority students in a number of settings and ways: in classrooms and the library, to be sure, but also through sensitivity in relation to the campus food service, student activities, student gathering places, the registration process, the availability and quality of advising and counseling, and the ways supplementary academic assistance is made available and presented;

■ developing "interest groups" for minority students as early as their sophomore year, linking them with representatives of fields they might enter after college—business and industry, education, public-service organizations, and the like—and, through summer internships, provide them with hands-on experience in those areas;

■ ensuring, where language mastery remains a problem, that English-as-a-second-language programs are available and utilized.

There is another set of on-campus activities designed to engage minority employees more fully and to make their success more likely. These may be called "faculty and staff development activities," and include:

■ giving priority in faculty and staff hiring to minority/bilingual/crosscultural persons;

■ encouraging links with universities to give priority in doctoral admission to qualified minority state college graduates with master's degrees;

■ supporting minority faculty and staff, financially or through released time, in negotiating the next steps in their careers: completing the doctorate, finishing a manuscript, attending institutes, and participating in further study;

■ reflecting the college's commitment to equity for minorities and the elimination of minority underrepresentation in its establishment of priorities, decision making, hiring practices, resource allocation,

reward structures, and institutional procedures for auditing progress toward these goals.

Finally, there is a group of activities that, successfully implemented, could strengthen the ties between colleges and other institutions in society. Let "business" stand as the emblem for these other institutions, although they could include service clubs, not-for-profit arts groups, and—in some settings—organized religious groups. The concept here is to convince "business" (or the other institutions) that it has a deep stake in the successful education of its community's minorities through college level. A variety of helpful activities could flow from this conviction:

- initiating "adopt-a-(minority)-student" programs at either the high school or college level. By participating in these programs, minority students could be introduced to the life of "business" through school work or internships, paid vacation-time jobs in the business, and association with employees at all levels in the business—support of a psychological as well as, perhaps, financial nature, a kind of initiation by business of students into its culture and work;

- making available "business" managers at a variety of levels to conduct periodic workshops and courses on high school and college campuses. These "on-loan" managers (the nature, extent, and duration of whose "loan" could vary tremendously) might initiate leadership training sessions in their areas of special knowledge, manifesting the commitment of "business" to the recruitment of minority employees and facilitating the entry of the minority college or university graduate into the work of the institution;

- making available to minority students, or organized groups of minority students on campus, equipment and funds as well as expertise and training experiences;

- encouraging "businesses" to emulate the recently announced program of Boston's major corporations to facilitate—even guarantee—access to college for the city's high school graduates, and subsequently to facilitate transition into the labor market through guaranteed employment. This program may prove to be a powerful, farsighted model for cities with large numbers of minority and low-income families.

Campuses could establish constructive links with virtually all of the environing institutions. Such alliances could not fail to have salutary effects on minority students by strengthening their competencies, bolstering their confidence level, and, ultimately, their degree of success.

Higher Education Governing Boards

Reams have been written about the powerful, pivotal roles of higher education governing boards. That theme, though not developed here, is an undeniable fact. Governing boards can make things happen and prevent things from happening. Because the members of public college and university boards are political appointees, or are sometimes elected by the public, the boards tend to reflect a state's current political mood. Because of the practice in many states of extended terms, there are, however, notable positive exceptions. Boards have been known to challenge prevailing sentiment, to serve as the conscience of the campus and the state. Boards have called upon campuses to quicken sensitivity, to rekindle efforts, to initiate needed programs.

Boards are overwhelmingly more likely to reflect sensitivity to the realities of minorities—and to call for action programs that ensure their inclusion in higher education—when persons of minority backgrounds serve on them. There is a vividness to experience that eclipses imagination and good intention alone. A minority member can often remind fellow board members of why constructive action is necessary because he or she *knows* the need and feels its urgency. It is in the interests of all that board membership be diversified in terms of gender, age, life experience, and background. Hence it is necessary, as well as appropriate, to do everything possible to ensure that persons of minority backgrounds are appointed to these governing bodies.

The Challenge

Now is a golden opportunity for America to reaffirm its commitment to the education of all its citizens. That dream took years to crystallize. This is the century in which it should be realized.

America can ill afford not to achieve the educational empowerment of its people. It is, to be sure, a matter of equity. It is also the only way in which this country will be resourceful, competitive, and strong.

"From cradle to grave," Henry Adams wrote, "this problem of running order through chaos, direction through space, discipline through freedom, unity through multiplicity has always been, and must always be, the task of education as it is the moral of religion, philosophy, science, art, politics, and economy." The brilliance, as well as the truth, of this passage lies in its linking education with the other great human realities—religion, science, art, politics, economics. This essay has dwelt on only one dimension, albeit an essential one, of education: achieving "unity through multiplicity."

The Greeks made a basic distinction between a form or level of education for citizens with civic responsibility to govern ("liberal arts") and another ("servile education") for those who needed some education in their work but who did not share in the responsibility for public affairs.

Poised just a decade-plus from the twenty-first century, we know that the coming era will require that virtually all citizens be educated, in the Greek sense, in "the liberal arts," for each must assume the responsibilities of citizenship. There is no room for servility. Below the calm surfaces of the national and international scene lie challenges, troubles, and turbulence that will demand the utmost discernment, courage, and wisdom.

The age demands a citizenry capable of creating and sustaining a world fit for free persons. The American people will not be able to meet that responsiblity unless they are educated. Our challenge is clearly to find ways to achieve "unity through multiplicity," to engage, sustain, and make higher education available to *all* of America's people.

Notes

[1]The following sections draw upon Reginald Wilson and Sarah E. Melendez, Minorities in Higher Education: Fifth Annual Status Report (Washington, DC: American Council on Education, 1986).

[2]National Center for Education Statistics, U.S. Dept. of Education, Special Report, November 1983, pp. 3-4; Reginald Wilson and Sarah E. Melendez, "Down the Up Staircase," *Educational Record*, Fall 1985, pp. 46-50.

[3]*Chronicle of Higher Education*, 23 July 1986.

[4]Brent Staples, "The Dwindling Black Presence on Campus," *New York Times Magazine*, 27 April 1986, pp. 46, 50, 52, 54, 62.

[5]*Chronicle of Higher Education*, 10 Sept. 1986, p. 1.

3

Standing at the Crossroads: Traditionally Black Colleges Today

Albert N. Whiting
Former Chancellor
North Carolina Central University

Sociology teaches that society contains in-groups and out-groups and that the attitude of an in-group member toward those in the out-group is inevitably negative and/or hostile and vice versa. It also teaches that social devices such as segregation and their accompanying rationale tend to highlight in a derogatory manner the characteristics of the out-groups that differ from those of the in-group. Thus, the in-group tends to generalize as negative all the major traits associated with the out-group, almost always basing these generalizations on perceptions of intergroup contrast. Consequently, given the history of the United States, with its deep ethnocentric tendencies, anything rooted and initiated in the American black community is, even in these days, considered automatically inferior. From this base it is an easy progression for majority members to ask, "Why do we need black colleges if segregation is officially dead and if our national goal is integration?"

There are today ninety-nine traditionally black institutions (TBIs). Prior to 1976 there were 105; but between 1976 and 1984, five of these closed—all were private and all but one were two-year institutions.[1] Of the 100 current TBIs, eighty-nine award baccalaureate or postbaccalaureate degrees and eleven are two-year colleges. Fifty-seven are privately controlled, and all but twelve of these have religious affiliations. Forty-three are publicly supported institutions, and it is significant to note that these account for over two-thirds of the total enrollment in the TBIs, which in 1980, the peak year, was approximately 222,000 and somewhat less than this in 1982. Between 1980 and 1982 there was a visible drop in black enrollment in the TBIs, which had been more or less stable from 1976 to 1980. This decline, however, was partially offset by small but steady increases in "other race" and foreign students. Historically, TBIs have always been open to nonblacks and foreign students, but these students have now become a surprisingly significant part of TBI enrollments. In fact, in 1982 one out of every five TBI students was white, Hispanic, Asian, American Indian, or nonresident alien, totaling about 40,000 for all the TBIs.

Early Development of TBIs

Higher education institutions for blacks were founded and developed under a condition unlike that of other colleges and

universities in this country: as a result of segregation, official separation from the national system of higher education. The effort emerged at first largely out of the interests of private groups—the black communities, philanthropists, freedmen's societies, and Northern-based churches. Later, Reconstruction state governments organized public school systems for both blacks and whites, but after Reconstruction, per-pupil expenditures for blacks fell, and schools were placed so as not to facilitate educational opportunities for blacks. Consequently, long years after the Civil War, private groups still provided the major educational opportunities for blacks at all levels. Most of the black colleges, under the aegis of these private groups, began by offering high school-level work out of necessity while slowly evolving as college-level institutions.

In 1915, for example, a federal report on black schools secondary and higher listed only three institutions as "college-grade": Howard University, Meharry Medical College, and Fisk University. Thirty other black institutions offered some college-level work but were not described as "college-grade" because of the size of their high school departments. All of the institutions at this time offering some college-level work were private, other than a land-grant college and a state college.

A follow-up federal study in 1927 reported considerable improvement in public secondary school provisions for black and, as a result, many of the private colleges had phased out their high school departments, leaving them free to concentrate on college-level offerings. By this time there were seventy-seven institutions offering collegiate work—an increase of forty-four over those indicted in the 1915 study. This large increase resulted primarily from the emergence of the black college public sector.

A third federal survey in 1942 indicated that black colleges had improved considerably more—in fact to the point where undergraduate offerings in the public black and white colleges were fairly comparable. There was, however, an expected disparity in graduate-level offerings, which the black schools really did not attempt to establish until after the 1935 challenge of the "separate but equal" doctrine noting that there was a lack of public graduate and professional schools for blacks in those states with dual systems of education. These states, incidentally, were ones in which the great majority of the black population was located. Afterward, six private black schools in 1936 organized graduate programs, but none of the public institutions offered work at this level. During all of this period states with dual systems made funds available for blacks to pursue graduate and/or professional studies in nondual system states. Such arrangements were never adequate in terms of facilitating access and opportunity.

After World War II, federal financial assistance to attend college became available on a wide scale. The GI Bill had veterans flocking to the campuses, and by 1947 in the black schools they constituted over one-third of the enrollment. Their presence continued in significant proportions through the 1950s and 1960s.

In 1954 the U.S. Supreme Court, in its *Brown* vs. *Board of Education* decision, declared "separate educational facilities inherently unequal." Just prior to this declaration black colleges had about 75,000 undergraduate students and about 3,200 graduate students and in that year awarded approximately 12,000 bachelor's and first professional degrees and about 1,300 master's degrees. For a while after this decision black students continued to attend TBIs at about the same rate as before. In 1961 black students had been admitted in small numbers to 17 percent of the public white institutions in the South. By 1965 it is estimated that admissions had risen to approximately 25 percent of all the black students in the South. By 1970 this figure had increased to 40 percent.

At the same time that this shift was occurring TBIs were enrolling increasing numbers of black students, although the rate of increase was smaller. Obviously, both TBIs and traditionally white institutions (TWIs) were drawing black students from an expanding number of black high school graduates who were benefiting from federal financial aid programs (BEOG, SEOG, NDSL, guaranteed student loans, etc.) and improved parental incomes.

In 1970 the Legal Defense Fund of the National Association for the Advancement of Colored Persons (NAACP) filed a class action suit (*Adams*) against the federal government to enforce desegregation of public higher education. Litigation continued throughout the seventies with the ultimate result being the requirement that public black colleges

and universities be enhanced and that black enrollment and faculty be increased at the white colleges. Thus the 1970s became a major transition period that set in motion significant trends in enrollment, degree production, curricula, finance, employee mix, and the role of both the TBIs and TWIs.

The Picture at Present

Because of the Court's mandate requiring the TWIs to increase their minority enrollments, the most notable trend of the 1970s was a disproportionate shifting of black students out of the TBIs in response to the lure of generous scholarships, stepped-up recruiting efforts, and the opportunity to study at larger, more prestigious institutions with a wider array of academic offerings. This shift started largely with the brightest students first and then filtered down to the more average group. By 1980 this process left the TBIs with only 37 percent of all black students in colleges and universities in the United States, and according to recent estimates this figure is now about 20 percent.[3] It should be noted again, however, that while this shift was occurring it was slightly offset by an increase in enrollment at the TBIs of "other race" and ethnic groups (i.e., whites, Asians, Indians, Hispanics, and nonresident aliens). In fact these students accounted for a total of 40,000 in TBI enrollments in 1982, or approximately one out of every five students, and whites represented about 11 percent of all TBI students, enrolled mostly as part-time students and largely in the graduate and professional programs.

A second trend stimulated by the 1970s was a broadening in TBI curricula and degree production from education and social science largely to business administration and management, engineering, public affairs, and health. In addition, considerably more attention was given to the development of graduate-level work—master's and doctoral. Prior to the 1970s only Howard University, Atlanta University, and, at one time, North Carolina Central University, conferred doctoral degrees. During the 1970s, three others introduced such programs in this period—Texas Southern, Meharry, and Jackson State—and an additional three—Morgan State University, University of Maryland Eastern Shore, and Tennessee State—started doctoral programs in 1982.

A third trend, perhaps not as noticeable as the other two, relates to finances. Overall TBI revenues increased approximatley 50 percent between 1971 and 1981. This resulted mostly from an increase in state appropriations and federal funds. But there was also an increase in tuition and fees plus a small increase in gifts, grants and endowment funds—enough at least to keep up with rising inflation. Enhancement funds related to the *Adams* case decision were extremely helpful in the public sector in broadening degree offerings, improving academic equipment and resources and, in general, lifting the TBI institutions above their historic marginal levels. Although the private TBIs did not share in the enhancement funds, they did profit from the increased state programs of aid to private colleges. During this period, a number of states developed programs of aid for their private colleges. These programs provided state funds based on a number of in-state students the colleges enrolled. Without these infusions of money the marginality of the private TBIs would have accentuated, the quality would have declined, and their competitiveness would have been seriously reduced, particularly in light of the rampant inflation of this period.

Then finally the widening of federal and state student aid enabled the TBIs to maintain and even increase enrollments as the pool of black high school graduates widened and as access broadened to include students from the lower economic levels. In the historically black institutions, participation in these aid programs was extremely high, sometimes involving as many as eight out of every ten students for the BEOG and roughly three out of ten in the SEOG and Work Study programs. Another program, although not set in motion by the events of the 1970s, was the Title III grant program which was designated originally for "developing institutions" (i.e., black) and later retitled as the program for "underfinanced institutions." Established by the Higher Education Act of 1965, this program proved strategically sustaining for the TBIs because through it they received fairly generous grants for curricular improvements, management and development training, remedial programs, faculty improvement, and various special needs. Without this assistance, the TBIs in many instances would have lost whatever competitive quality they had attained. It should be noted, however, that at a point when their future is in greatest jeopardy the TBIs

are now losing some Title III funds as other minority and underfinanced majority schools qualify for participation.

Reference must also be made to the "catch-up" funds many of the "Adams states" appropriated for the public-sector TBIs during the 1970s, most in response to "consent decree" agreements in the wake of the *Adams* decision. These funds were of invaluable assistance in boosting these colleges and universities to funding levels approximating (in some instances equaling) those of the majority institutions. Although this measure was undoubtedly helpful, it could not compensate for years of underfunding and the concomitant sociopsychological conditions. Nevertheless these infusions of funds, in situations where there was already a quality potential, resulted in a surge of competitiveness that was, at the outset, inherent in the plan for enhancement.

While the public-sector TBIs experienced a measure of financial "prosperity" during the 1970s, the private-sector schools, even with the newly gained state institutional aid for in-state students, seemed to be going downhill. In contrast to the state-supported schools their enrollment decline was not offset by a significant increase in "other race" students and an array of new ethnic attendees. Consequently in the United Negro College Fund group 50 percent consistently lost enrollment between 1979 and 1983. In addition, faculty salaries lagged behind the national average, making it difficult for these schools to attract top-notch scholars and/or to retain well-qualified people. In 1983-84 the average salary for a professor was $22,735; associate professor $18,721; assistant professor $16,570; instructor $14,354. Endowment funds did not grow much—just barely equaling the rise in inflation—and revenues overall just barely met expenditures. In 1981-82 endowment funds for the forty-two schools totaled $147,193,589, with an average per-institution figure of $3,504,609. In the next year the figures were $201,339,125, with an average of $4,793,789. However, it should be noted that over half of these funds are held by six schools. With regard to overall revenues and expenditures the former in 1981-82 was, for the total group, $334,085,500 while the latter was $336,510,970, reflecting a deficit of roughly 2.5 million, while in 1982-83 the revenue was $355,396,812 and expenditures were $334,607,640, showing a surplus for the group of approximately $10.5 million.[4] Figures are not immediately available on capital expenditures but at this moment there is a rather large deferred maintenance problem at many of the institutions. At one of the better known of this group, the physical plant is in an appalling condition, with no prospect for immediate attention. Thus the overall picture is indeed bleak.

The Future

Throughout the nation, in both majority and black communities, public comment on the future of the TBIs reflects a rather deep ambivalence. This feeling may result from reservations still existing in the minds of many about the nation's degree of commitment to integration. Limits to access and the lack of comfortable absorption of blacks in majority situations tend to encourage minority suspicion and to maintain a feeling of social distance on the part of the majority member. This problem is worsened by practices or strategems that heighten visibility (e.g., black dormitories on white campuses, black student unions) or out-group status. Until black-white interaction can occur within the framework of sympathetic person-to-person relations rather than in terms of group symbols with historic baggage, full integration will not be achieved.

As Jacqueline Fleming has suggested, Blacks in College, a significant though declining number of black students will still gravitate toward black colleges because of the psychosocial comfort they afford.[5] She avers that the black schools provide a more positive, more meaningful education for blacks than do counterpart white colleges. She also argues that TBIs still educate a significant proportion of black students, despite a decline in the number of black students attending black schools, and still confer a disproportionately high share of the degrees. (This was more true in the 1970s than in the 1980s.) In fact, by 1981 TWIs awarded two-thirds of the baccalaureate degrees received by black students.[6] Therefore, part of the public's ambivalence about TBIs may relate to thinking based on what was rather than what is.

What do present and former presidents and chancellors of TBIs have to say about these institutions? The variety and ambivalence in their comments poignantly illustrate that TBIs are now finding themselves at a crossroads.

A former president of a prominent, private TBI institution as long ago as 1935, retired for many years but still active in educational matters, says that "the elimination of segregation and the development of equality was not an overnight process. If we had at once eliminated segregation by closing all the black schools, we would have also denied access to higher education to a very high percentage of black youngsters. These youngsters had neither the money nor the educational qualifications to enter the traditionally white schools. Nor were these schools ready to receive large numbers of black students. For a period after the Supreme Court decision of 1954, segregation was eliminated in name only. The decision opened a modicum of opportunity for a few black students in traditionally white institutions, but for most blacks the doors remained closed. During the early stages of desegregation the black colleges continued to provide educational opportunities to the masses of black youngsters. I think, therefore, that we have made more progress because the black institutions persisted and grew than we would have had without them. If they had been suddenly eliminated, I think we would have had more hardship, fewer students, and more unsatisfactory academic race relations than we have had.

"I think that we would have now moved to the stage that we are now ready to view integration as a two-way street. Even Earl McGrath noted that he found some white schools that were just as bad as some black ones, but he also noted that for many people, educational opportunity was also a matter of availability. So we now see the pendulum swinging back toward the black schools as a resource because of finances, geography, and availability as we have of white schools being an opportunity for black students. As black schools, both public and private, have improved the quality of their offerings and expanded them, white students have taken advantage of the opportunity the black schools offer.

"Unfortunately, some whites have not yet given up the struggle to eliminate the black college, and wherever they could plant a branch of the main university of agricultural and technical college in the same community where a black college had existed for years, they have done so. Huntsville, Alabama, is a prime example of that. These machinations have hindered the full development of integration and equal opportunity for both blacks and whites.

"Another difficulty is that some of the changes seem to be going too far for both blacks and whites, as in the case of West Virginia, where a previously black school has become almost completely a white one. I suppose that in the case of the black public colleges, there is still this battle going on as to how much opportunity they will be permitted to offer, as in the blocking of North Carolina A & T College from starting a school of veterinary medicine. We still have not faced up to the most economical, feasible, and humane way to bring about successful integration. But I am convinced that the more we strengthen the black institution and make it more nearly the equal of similar opportunities in the predominantly white institutions, the more integration will take place as a two-way street, with movement in both directions.

"Some [black schools] should go out of existence. I think the time for us to worship at the shrine of blackness without quality is over. The sooner we get over that, the better. But as long as we can improve the quality of our institutions so that they represent a professional need, I don't believe we need many Ph.D. programs. I really think the primary role of the black college now—and I would say this is particularly true of the private but you may say it is also true of the public—is at the undergraduate level—the strongest undergraduate education we can give so that our young people then will have access and competence at the graduate and the professional level."

A president who served in the late 1960s, 1970s, and early 1980s, first in a private TBI and later in the public sector, says:

"I think that the future is very dark. I don't see that many of these schools are going to survive as predominantly black institutions. I think they are going to become predominantly white or be merged out of existence, the public ones particularly. There are two or three reasons. One is a high per capita cost in these institutions when legislators have begun to talk about economies. Another is the talk about duplication of effort and duplication of courses. Then there is the *Adams* vs. *Richardson* plus similar cases. The amounts of money these institutions need to enhance them or to bring them up to the *Adams* level will cost most of the *Adams* states more money than they are willing to put into the schools. That is what I really believe. Finally, I also think that the black colleges really are going to be the cause of their own death because they are trying to do too many things with too few resources to meet too

many demands made on them and because they are not really living up to the standards they should be living up to.

"[This problem is] the result of social change. I think that the presidents would be considered Judases if they publicly expressed such an analysis. (If I were to say some of these things in a public forum or in a group of alumni, I would probably be either lynched or run out!) You and I know that to do what we feel is the best thing for these institutions in many cases cannot be done and the institution would not survive because we are not going to get the kind of help we are talking about. We are not going to get the kind of faculty we are talking about. We are not going to get the kinds of students needed at this time. We have got a lot of work to be done, and it's going to be tough."

A president of a public institution in a large, urban area, who has been in office about fifteen years, says:

"The role of the historically black school during the days of segregation as against this period of desegregation is essentially the same. And we're not talking about remediation. I understand we have the role of remediation, you know we're the best there, accelerating the learning process of people and getting them out when they come from backgrounds that are so poor because of the poor urban schools systems, or what have you. That is a role that we continue to play. But that's also the role that people want to use to say, 'Well, the community colleges can do that.' But remediation is a small part of the total role that the black college plays. And the black college plays as much of a significant role now as it did in 1900—of developing professionals.

"A cosmopolitan campus, a campus that reflects in reasonable proportion the races and the gender of all students with some foreign students, is as excellent an environment for the black student to be exposed to on a black college campus as it is for white students to be exposed to on a white college campus. So I would be interested in integration from the point of view of black students having a wider exposure to people of, if I may use the term, of subculture groups.

"Integration can take place at both ends of the spectrum. I believe a minority group of white students on a black college campus is integration. Now I believe that the black college ought to be a place that black students can come, get a good solid academic training, learn leadership, what leadership means, and while they are on that particular campus, be able to shore up an emotional armor to deal with the hard, tough society and environment that they are going to meet when they get out. I think that the black college has to continue to be this kind of place. It has to continue to make sure that Langston Hughes and Paul Lawrence Dunbar and Frederick Douglass and Julian Percy and all these people continue to live within this country as well as to live internationally. So I am in the category of those who want to preserve black colleges for blacks, I do not see a black college changing to a white college. I believe though that once 50 percent of the student body becomes white, it becomes very difficult to hold the line. Something becomes wrong with the administration and something is wrong with the faculty and so on, and that's the way it is.

"The black college has to be competitive. If it has a good solid academic program, is a well-managed and efficiently operated institution, has a clear set of goals that fits in with a mission that is understood, and establishes reasonable enrollment estimates and projections and has the enrollment necessary to generate the funds required to keep the enterprise going, I think, then, that the black college can make it. I feel deeply that we can compete with anybody within the scope and role of the mission that we have. We will get our admissions people working and we will give our competitors a run for their money. Just because we are predominantly black, we're not going to take the position that we can't come up to snuff. Oh, the racism will always hurt us to some extent, but if we are good enough, we'll be able to overcome enough of that—not all of it, but enough to survive. But it does require, I think, lining up all of these things. Now the one danger would be the great dependency on student financial aid. I see that as the greatest threat to all for us. So my role has to be to find whatever way that I can to develop great skill in raising funds to try to help our foundation board get enough funds so that we can have a big enough endowment to provide enough loans and scholarships to keep our enrollment going if the student financial aid structure collapses. Failure to have these back-up funds could be devastating.

"We made a conscious decision that we are not going to establish enrollment projections beyond 1,900 FTE a year. But we know that we

can reach 1,900. If we can keep the student financial aid thing in check until we can get enough independent scholarships, 1,900 FTE will secure our survival. If we established our goal, our projections at 4,500 FTE we would be writing our own demise because we could probably come up with only 3,500 if we shuffled and scrambed for every warm body we found.

"It is a possibility that we could have gotten a bit ambitious, overly ambitious. We have a lot of faculty members who would want the projection to be set at 3,000 FTE because we would get more funds. We're enrollment driven, so that we can temporarily get more funds by projecting higher enrollments. We did not want to be tempted in that direction so we set ours back. So as long as we make our enrollment, we can deal well with the accrediting bodies. White institutions can afford to say, 'We're not going to go with outside accreditation, we don't want this, we don't think the agencies are any good.' We as black institutions cannot afford to do that. We must be able at all times to say that we have met minimum requirements of the professional societies and agencies. Accreditation knocks out some of that tendency to judge us as inferior. But in any event, if those things are in line, I firmly believe we can compete. If we can compete, then we will give the university and everybody else a run for their money."

A retired president who was in office for thirteen years, in a state-supported institution located in a Northen state about thirty miles from a large, metropolitan area, says:

"Yes, the historically black college is necessary. Unequivocally so. I reflect each time that question is asked. I say, those who ask the question with a serious intent of trying to get a 'no' from a person are really asking whether the educational system is necessary, and they will all deny that. On another level, those who ask that question may be saying that every person in the American complex can arrive at his or her full potential through a single type of institution, and that is not my belief.

"Segregation still persists in this state. There was legal segregation until almost the time of the *Brown* decision. Now the role, then and now, our black colleges has is the all-important traditional mission of inspiring, through role models, our students. We had then, and we have now, the understanding of the problems of the black student. We had then, and we have now, the need for expressing that problem. We had then and now a need for a student to see and believe that he can obtain the status that is reflected in the hierarchy of a black school, or certainly in the hierarchy of the graduates of that black school.

"Essentially, I don't see any difference in the TBI role whether determined by segregation or desegregation, but I see one additional burden that is placed on the black school today. That black school has to be more than certain that our holocaust is not forgotten.

"In the light of my experiences—thirteen years as president—and in the light of what I saw as a basic need, our schools must be certain that they are competitive in programmatic thrust and certainly programmatic in the outcome, in the productive outcome of our graduates. Whatever graduates we produce must be able to enter the competitive market, make progress and know that he or she has a realistic shot at the top job in that hierarchy.

"[But] we have to revise our approaches. In the revised approaches you have to come head-on with the fact that there are those who think that if the black colleges, the few black businesses that we have, the few professionals that we have, would just go away, we would be in the land of Utopia. There's no Utopia, unless all the people have some or all of the bounties of that nation. So we've got to have projection of competency to its utmost—having every graduate be a competent, competitive professional. We have to work for that.

The next thing, we have to know, is that society is becoming more conservative, and we are going to have to find ways and means of getting things done. What do I mean by that? There are 114 black colleges—historically black colleges and universities. There are at least 5,000 black churches in this nation. It might be possible for a cadre of churches to adopt our schools and to pour money into those schools. We've got to find ways and means to get our businesses to adopt and to pour money into schools. We've got to get to the fact or we've got to work our ways and means, rather, to get to the fact that those of us who have money must be willing to and must make investments in the black enterprises. I'll take Philadelphia, for example. One basketball player on the Sixers has a reputed salary of $2 million, and if he gave $500,000 of that to a

cadre of black colleges, his net take-home will not be changed much. We've got to do that.

Then we've got to tackle our alumni and get our alumni to know, and especially those of my generation, that without that black college they wouldn't have what they have, and they must pour something into a university or college on a consistent basis. And then, as a Pepsi Cola rep stated, we've got to change our marketing strategy, in substance, in imagery. And the major change, as I see it is, we can no longer go back to 'Here we are, aren't we poor.' "

A president of a prominent, private college in a large urban area, who has been in office from 1967 to the present, says:

"I think the historically black school is very necessary for a number of reasons. In the first place, black students need schools that can care for them. I have not yet seen a predominantly white institution that is as caring and concerned about black students as the black colleges are. The black student has a friend in the black college that he does not have in the predominantly white institution. So that is one thing right off the bat. Another thing is that there are many black students who are much more comfortable in the black college than they are in the predominantly white college. In the next place, a black college breeds confidence in the black student. Many students come to the black college without confidence and without hope, and they get built up to the point that they are able to compete successfully in graduate and professional schools after they complete their work in the black private colleges.

"Another big advantage is that the black college focuses on the racial background and problems of black students. [At my institution,] for example, we give a great deal of attention to the African and Afro-American backgrounds of our students and we develop a knowledge and understanding of those backgrounds, and we develop ways in which to tackle problems which are peculiar to those backgrounds. Another advantage of the black college is that it encourages a knowledge and understanding of African and Afro-American culture. All of this adds up to indicate that a black college is generally more caring and because it more caring it can develop a black student, in my opinion, much more successfully than an integrated school can, a predominantly white school can.

"White colleges that used to be closed to black students are now opened and the white public colleges, those that used to be all white back in the days of segregation, are now open, and they are drawing from the black colleges students who used to go to black public and private colleges. In addition the predominantly white private colleges are admitting black students in considerable numbers, too, if they can pay. And so you see a large number of black students now going to expensive predominantly white schools like Duke and Emory and Tulane. So we are in a new day now, a day of integration as opposed to a day of segregation in the earlier years. Under the impact of a situation in which the doors to predominantly white colleges are now open we have certain peculiar problems at the black colleges. The first problem we have is that white students are not moving into black colleges normally unless they have to. If the black college is the only alternative, or if it is the better alternative, then white students will go to the black college.

"I'm speaking in terms of the *accessibility*, and this accessibility is draining enrollment. So in the situation where black colleges are available and accessible, white students are not moving to them in large numbers unless they have no other options or unless their options are not attractive. On the other hand, black students are moving in very large numbers into white schools that were previously closed. White students are not moving into the black colleges because of precedent and prejudice. In the first place, they are not accustomed to going to the black colleges and in the second place some of them are uncomfortable in black colleges no matter how strong these black colleges may be. So we are in a situation in which there is a heavy outflow of black students into the predominantly white schools and a very limited inflow of white students into the predominantly black institutions.

"Now that situation plus inflation and unemployment and decreasing financial aid have caused considerable problems in the black colleges. The black colleges that are very, very hard hit are generally in two classifications; one, those that are located in small towns are having a hard time; second, those that are poorly managed are having difficulties; and so we see declining enrollment in the black colleges that

are located in small towns as well as the poorly managed black colleges that are located in cities, and so we have declining enrollments in the urban black colleges which have been poorly managed. Now the stronger black colleges in the urban centers are getting along just as well as the white institutions in those centers. For example, I would say that Hampton and Morehouse and Spelman are examples of schools that are thriving. We have five applicants for every one position here at [my institution]. We have a dormitory room shortage. We have 500 students living in the city who would like to live on the campus. And I would say that the peculiar problems and handicaps are not facing all of our colleges but they are facing most of them."

Returning now to the question posed at the outset: What is the value of traditionally black institutions in a society committed to integration? Do we need black colleges today? Comments from blacks range from an emotional, unequivocal, uncritical "yes" to a "yes" qualified by the realities of our time. Many of the private TBIs are so operationally marginal in terms of finances, students, academic resources, physical plant, faculty and support staff that their continued existence and educational effectiveness in terms of today's standards are questionable. The public institutions, on the other hand, are for the most part operationally viable but have their legitimacy questioned on the assumption that dual provisions are no longer needed, that duplication is wasteful, and that dismantling is considered legally and socially desirable. Recognizing these facts, pragmatic supporters of black schools accept the inevitability of the closing of TBIs where vulnerability is high—both private and public—especially where enrollments have dwindled below critical masses and where duplication by other geographically proximate public institutions makes defense of the schools improbable.

In the white community there is similar sentiment but more negative in tone. Some, perhaps many, feel that minority institutions are unqualifiedly inferior and therefore, in a desegregated society, unnecessary. Others, including those attending the TBIs, recognize and appreciate the utility of the more competitive, outreaching TBIs but tend to feel that a number have outlived their historic role.

As our overall population increases and as life in the United States becomes more complex, more dependent on technology, more "demassified," there will be a continued need for a diverse array of institutions, including educational ones. Alvin Toffler makes this point in a more general way in *The Third Wave*: "The answer to these problems . . . lies in imaginative new arrangements for accommodating and legitimating diversity—new institutions that are sensitive to the rapidly shifting needs of changing and multiplying minorities."[7] Demographic projections for the year 2020 indicate that one out of three working adults will be a minority person (i.e., black and/or Hispanic).[8] In other words, America is becoming less white. With the experience that TBIs developed through the years in educating minority, underprepared, culturally deprived poor, it is obvious that there is a role for their kind of educational expertise and empathy. In another sense, also, and within the type of social structure visualized by Toffler, an integrated society in the future will have to be based on the acceptance of the concept of cultural pluralism.

During this period of transition from segregation to desegregation there is still evidence of resistance—covert, to be sure in most instances—to an all-out commitment to the idea and ideal of integration. For example, of the nineteen states under federal orders to desegregate their public colleges, only six have more black undergraduates enrolled at public institutions now than they did in 1980. In the remaining thirteen states black enrollment in the public colleges has declined.[9] Both the states and the federal government obviously have now made commitment to integration an agenda of relatively low priority. The result may well be that fewer blacks are now receiving higher education in these states. If no TBIs existed at all in these same states, educational access and opportunity for blacks would be significantly reduced. To be fair, it should be noted that this indictment represents an assessment made without an analysis of the extent to which the overall decline in black college attendance is reflected in these figures. Nevertheless it is difficult to escape the gut feeling that the dynamics and momentum of the integration movement have waned.

On the other hand, in at least four instances clearly and in many others marginally, TBIs have become high-percentage, white-attended institutions—a logistical accommodation of profound social significance. It is possible that this development could occur on a wider scale in the future if "market forces," so to speak, are allowed to prevail freely. This possibility is a strong argument, we believe, to reason against a *categorical* approach to the question: Do we need black colleges?

However, many blacks, because of their internalization of their out-group status, are not functionally or psychologically comfortable in a white majority environment. For them, black colleges provide a bridge that fosters intellectual self-confidence and quickened maturation, enabling them to proceed either to further education in graduate or professional school or to professional service with greater efficiency and strengthened by a sense of worth. Until society becomes more of an inclusive in-group, there will still be an important educational role for schools such as the TBIs. This role should persist through at least another generation (i.e., thirty to forty years).

Until ethnocentrism and racism in this country and in high places are greatly reduced, if not eliminated, the predominantly black school must be continued in order to transmit to society and to its students— though a rapidly dwindling number—the elements, the tone, the ethos of the Afro-American subculture, its contributions to the larger American culture, and its identification through transfusion and acculturation with other cultures of the world. Majority institutions, while moving recently in this direction, still tend to fuse the Afro-American subculture with a Western cultural perspective that leads to selectivity and an awkward or overly indulgent interpretation of its essential elan.

What, then, is the present and future value of TBIs, and what should be done to preserve them?

- TBIs have played a historically imperative role, under the most difficult circumstances, in the education of black people in the– United States and should be commended for accomplishing this role in heroic fashion.

- Until the national commitment to integration is unequivocally firm, TBIs will be strategically useful in providing full-range access to those minority students whose needs, at this point, are better satisfied in a TBI setting.

- Recognition should be given to the fact that, increasingly, some TBIs, because of location, offerings, and delivery systems, are logistically significant in providing educational opportunities for the majority as well as the minority community.
- The expertise TBIs have developed in the teaching of the underprepared and culturally deprived will be strategically useful as the minority population of this country increases.
- TBIs that meet regional accreditation standards and are, therefore fully accredited should not have the stereotypical label of "inferiority" attached to them any more than TWIs evaluated under the same standards.
- Efforts to close TBIs simply because of racial identification should be opposed in favor of allowing natural history and market forces to run their course.
- An affirmative effort should be launched to publicize the "effectiveness" of the TBIs in terms of what they do for their students over a four- or five-year period, as measured in both academic and emotional growth.
- Provisions should be made through higher education associations to develop special programs in the areas of budgeting, management and development, and trusteeship to help TBIs bring their personnel into mainstream practices.

Notes

[1]Susan Hill, *The Traditionally Black Institutions of Higher Education* 1860-1982 (Washington, DC: National Center for Education Statistics), p. ix.

[2]The facts and figures for this section were taken largely from the study reported by Susan Hill, pp. ix-xix and pp. 1-40.

[3]*Black Enterprise*, November 1986, p. 24.

[4]The facts and figures on the UNCF Colleges are based on UNCF *Reports for* 1979-1983, Appendices A,G,M,N,R,V,S.

[5]Jacqueline Fleming, *Blacks in College* (San Francisco: Jossey Bass 1984).

[6]Michael Nettles and Joan C. Baratz, "Black Colleges: Do we Need them?" *Change*, March/April 1986, p. 58.

[7]Alvin Toffler, *The Third Wave* (New York: Bantom Books, 1981), p. 422.

[8]Harold L. Hodgkinson, *All One System: Demographics of Education, Kindergarten Through Graduate School* (Washington, DC: Institute of Educational Leadership, 1985), p. 3.

[9]*Chronicle of Higher Education*, 8 October 1986, pp. 43-44.